Chuckles and Challenges

Chuckles
and Challenges

Wit and Wisdom from a Child's World

Annetta E. Dellinger

BAKER BOOK HOUSE
Grand Rapids, Michigan 49506

To my gifts from God, John,
Douglas, and Laura Dellinger,
and the many beautiful little
preschoolers, their parents, and
my two assistants, Zelma and
Judy, who have been part of my
life at Trinity Lutheran School.
The smile I wear is because of the
JOY my heavenly Father has
given to me through *you,* his gift
of children!

I love *you* and Jesus too!

Contents

Tell Me All about Fathers

"When you have kids to tickle, you're a father."

"A father is someone who takes care of you, smiles at you, and gives your family love."

"When Daddy kisses me I feel things going ding-a-ling inside."

"Dads watch TV after they take naps."

"Dads take showers because they are men and can't fit in the tub."

Be wise, my son, and bring joy to my heart.
[Prov. 27:11]

Heavenly Father,
Being a parent is hard!
It is overwhelming when I realize *you* have given *me* the job of rearing children,
guiding them to develop good habits,
molding their character . . . wow, what a responsibility!

As much as I would like to take credit (most of the time) for my children, I can't. I am not always the kind,
loving,
forgiving parent
I should be.

I realize that without you, Father, I would make a real
     mess of my life
  and of my children, the future generation.

I want to give all glory to you, for
                              instantly being there each
                                        second
                                        of every
                                        day
     to help me deal with the multitudes of decisions
     I must make as a parent.

Thank you for recharging my run-down battery,
  so the energy of your Holy Spirit can flow from me
  to my children.

Thank you, Father, for living in my children.
It was you who led them to . . .
  come to the door and say, "We brought you some flowers
  because we love you," even if it was half the lilac tree!
  bring me iced tea on a hot afternoon — even if I was
  standing on the top of a ladder to paint the ceiling.
I love you for the gift of children.
I pray that others will see my family resemble you, our
     heavenly Father. Amen.

I Know All about Getting Married!

People get married . . .

> "when they have kids."
>
> "because they love each other."
>
> "so they can kiss on the lips."
>
> "because they are happy and nervous."

"You can find someone to marry if you look around in a restaurant, on the road, or in a house."

---

*Trust in the LORD with all your heart
and lean not on your own understanding; in all your
ways acknowledge him,
and he will make your paths straight.* [Prov. 3:5–6]

Dear all-knowing Lord,
   You knew I was in for a surprise!
   I soon found out that marriage was not always the glamorous, smooth path I dreamed of on my wedding day! Life soon became
                        a reality!

   Only you, Lord, have helped me to go on when I wanted to shout,

"I give up!"
Without you as the center of my family life I would have failed long ago!

I love you for the gift of children who have made my marriage complete and
for helping me stay on your path through
rough
and smooth times! Amen.

What Do Angels Do?

"Angels watch us, sit by us, pick up our sins and
take them to heaven."

"Angels have wings, one-half bird and one-half
person."

"Angels fly to angel school to learn."

"Angels live in angel land, it's way up north."

Angels fly around the sky when the moon is out and
guard people."

"Angels eat at God's house."

---

*For he will command his angels concerning you
to guard you in all your ways.* [Ps. 91:11]

Dear Jesus,
My shopping trip with the children was no different
than usual —

challenging!

I said all the usual things:
"No, you can't have that, it costs too much money!"
"Don't touch that, it will break!"

But this time, a new dimension was added to our excursion!
As I quickly tried to get only what was on my list and rushed
from aisle to aisle, the children disappeared!

13

I looked under the clothing racks . . .
　　I checked several nearby aisles . . .
　　　　they were nowhere in sight!

I felt my heart doing flip-flops.
My breathing rapidly increased.
I was frightened; could someone have taken them?

Dear Jesus, I thank you for sending your guardian angels to
watch over my children —

　　　　　　　　　no matter where they go,
　　　　　　　　　what they do, night or day,
　　　　　　　　　　they need your protection!

I am convinced that when you assigned my children guardian
angels, you knew exactly what you were doing! They can be
active and energetic little people!

Thank you, Jesus, for the gift of children and for your constant
loving protection. I love you. Amen.

What Is a Mommy?

"Someone who has babies pop out of her tummy."

"People who never have birthdays."

"You are a mommy when you learn to cook."

"Jesus makes you into a mommy."

"A mommy is someone who takes care of kids."

"Mothers tell you about Jesus when they tuck you into bed at night."

Her children arise and call her blessed. [Prov. 31:28]

Dearest Master,

To list all the things that a mother is or does is almost impossible — just like some days are — impossible!

Being a mother is . . .

putting kisses and bandages on invisible scratches
and praying for the broken arms!

proudly seeing pennies saved
and gladly loaning money for gas in the car!

receiving an abundance of kisses and hugs from the three-year-old
and a little peck on the cheek — occasionally — from the sixteen-year-old!

seeing your baby girl grow up and go to the prom!

seeing your tiny baby boy grow taller than his parents
and rear a family of his own!

15

praying she will be elected class secretary

and he will not be in a wreck!

working all day to prepare a balanced meal for the one night
this week when the entire family will be home; then
one child calls and says, "I have ball practice!" or
another says, "Yuk, is this all we are having?"

sewing for hours on the perfect outfit "like everyone else
has"

and having it worn once!

being so tired at the end of the day you wonder if they will
ever grow up

and then being rested and lonely because they have
grown and left home!

I often forget, Master, that you have given me my personal
mission field within my home. I am a witness twenty-four
hours each day—let my love for you shine through.

Thank you for the gift of children. I love you and pray that
someday they will say, "I want to be just like my mom and
dad!" Amen.

How Does Jesus Get People to Heaven?

"He pulls you up with his hands."

"Jesus pulls you up on the roof of the house and then pushes you into heaven."

"Jesus has a big jet plane and flies you into heaven."

"You have to die first."

"In my Father's house are many rooms. . . . I am going there to prepare a place for you." [John 14:2]

Dear Jesus,

Do you realize all the questions children ask parents about heaven?

Where is heaven?

Does it hurt to die?

Will I be bloody all over when I die?

If we go to heaven why do we need cemeteries?

Will there be a toyroom and a bedroom in heaven?

The list is endless!

Speak through me as I try to answer their questions.

Live in me that I may witness my faith in you and the joyful gift of eternal life.

Thank you for living in *our* home.
   Thank you for preparing a perfect heavenly home
      for each one of us.

Bless you, Father, for the gift of children and the opportunity
to lead them to love you more each day! I love you. Amen.

Why Couldn't They Put Humpty Dumpty Together Again?

"They tried but they couldn't get his body to stay
together."

"'Cause when the egg cracked it got all dirty."

"They didn't know where all the pieces were."

"They didn't hav any egg glue."

"Because they would get yolk all over their hands."

---

*"Whoever humbles himself like this child is the greatest in
the kingdom of heaven. And whoever welcomes a little child
like this in my name welcomes me."* [Matt. 18:4–5]

Dear Jesus,

Some days I feel like Humpty Dumpty . . . going to pieces!
The demands on my life — home, family, friends, social activities,

church, work — seem to pull the energy from my body in a
million directions!

I really like morning, Jesus, for then I know you have given
me another fresh start to continue through life on
earth.

I love the children you gave me. I would do anything for
    them . . .
  But, Jesus,
            could you please plan one day that I can "do my
                own thing . . ."
            read your Word and meditate without inter-
            ruptions.
            sit in the tub and relax with tons of bubbles
            without toys attacking me.
            have an evening out in an elegant restau-
            rant — candlelight, music, fancy foods —
            no burgers and fries.
            have time to read even one small magazine
            article without the phone ringing.

My life is like a puzzle!
            Each day a new piece is added.
                When you allow me to plan my day,
                    the pieces never fit exactly right!
                But, when I joyfully yield to you to complete
                    my day,
                    it's perfect!

Help me to see the challenge of being a parent is all part of
your perfect plan for my life. Thank you for someday complet-
ing my life's puzzle in your gift of Heaven.

Thank you
  for the gift of children who help to make my life a
            unique
                puzzle. I love you! Amen.

Tell Me about Jesus

"Jesus eats food like starfood, like the angels eat."

"Jesus' address is sky."

"Jesus is our very best friend."

"Jesus sometimes sends a big ladder for us to come to his house."

"Jesus picks us up when we die and takes us to heaven."

"Jesus always has a smile on his face 'cause he likes kids."

"Jesus' house looks like a cloud."

"Jesus wanted a big bed to sleep in so he bought one at Sears."

He took a little child and had him stand among them. Taking him in his arms, he said to them, "Whoever welcomes one of these little children in my name welcomes me; and whoever welcomes me does not welcome me but the one who sent me." [Mark 9:36–37]

Dear Jesus,

Thank you for taking us in your loving arms and gently touching our lives as we learn more about you.

Give us guidance as we search your Word and grow to intimately love you more each day!

It's a tremendous challenge . . .
but an exciting opportunity . . .
to know that you are having me care for your children.
Wow!

Put your arms around each of us and let us
explode with joy
as we tell others about you!
I love you for the gift of children. Amen.

Wrinkles

"You get wrinkles from dirt."

"You get rid of wrinkles by wiping them off with a white towel."

"You get them off your face by ironing them out."

"You can sew them up to get rid of them."

A happy heart makes the face cheerful. [Prov. 15:13]

Dear Father,

The commercial world around me is constantly bombarding me with the idea that I need to dress in expensive clothes, have the right figure, and wear all the right kinds of make-up to be attractive!

But, I feel differently . . .

I believe no matter how much time or money I spend on myself, the feeling in my heart is what will show on my face!

Thank you, Father, for the gift of inner beauty.

Help me to be attractive because *you* live in me!

Thank you, Father, for the gift of children to whom I can witness the beauty

of you. I love you. Amen.

Tell Me All You Know about Driving

"You have to be at least eight to drive."

"You have to be a big person."

"You can only drive when you are a daddy."

"A license tells you not to go fast."

"If they give you a ticket that means you can go to the ball game, I think!"

Search me, O God, and know my heart;
test me and know my anxious thoughts. [Ps. 139:23]

Dear precious Father,

I've heard the expression "do as I say, and not as I do" used quite often. As a parent,

I know exactly what it means!

When the children were little they heard me say, "At a stop sign you are supposed to stop!" "Obey the speed limit; it is for your safety!"

Now that they are grown up, they like to creep through stop signs and drive way over the speed limit.

I wonder where they learned that?!
Children definitely are mirrors of their parents!

Father, you know the desire in my heart to do what is right
and how much I want to obey your rules for life.

Yet, I often fail.

Thank you for forgiving me and for
giving me a fresh start again,

and again,

and again.

Thank you for giving even children insights to sort out the right
from the wrong and for making it through life

in spite of
what we mir-
ror to them.

I love you, precious and protecting Father, for the gift of children. Amen.

What Does the Cross Remind You Of?

"Jesus died for our sins."

"Love."

"Mother, 'cause she loves me."

"That Jesus is my friend."

"To tell the truth."

"Crosses say there is a church someplace."

"A cross is like an apple 'cause it gets worms in the wood, like the apple does."

Jesus said, "Let the little children come to me, and do not hinder them, for the kingdom of heaven belongs to such as these." [Matt. 19:14]

Dear Father,

It's been a long day!

Why is it only after the last child is put in bed and I'm ready to sit down and relax that one remembers he needs three dozen cookies for school tomorrow?

As I start down the stairs to fulfill this need, another child yells, "Bring me a drink, please, I'm thirsty,"

while yet another sweetly requests,

"Read me a Bible story, I like to hear about Jesus."

No matter how tired I am, or how much I want time to be me, never let me deny my children the privilege of hearing your Word or of learning of the overflowing love your Son Jesus demonstrated for us on the cross.

Help me
to be a demonstrator for you, Father.

Thank you for the gift of children . . . yes,

even when
I'm tired
I love them!

I love you too. Amen.

What Is a Church?

"Where people go and preach."

"Where I go to sing."

"Where they have bells to clang."

"It's white, big, and wide."

"Where you play in Sunday school."

"Churches have big triangles on top."

"Where you have to sit down and listen to stuff."

"A church is a place where my feet can't reach the floor."

"A place where Jesus lives."

"A church is full of crosses."

"A special friend's house."

Is any cheerful? Let him sing praise. [James 5:13, RSV]

Dear Jesus,

Why is Sunday a day of rest for everyone but me?

Today I managed to get almost everyone ready for church, complimented those who dressed themselves.

I tried to get matching gloves and boots on all the wiggly hands and feet . . .

took all the children to the bathroom between Sunday
school and church
and discovered one had forgotten to put on underwear!

By this time I was really looking forward to the hour with you.

Could I rest and praise you? Yes, Lord, yes!
As I listened to the children sing their own tunes of praise to
you . . .
I mentally hugged each one, smiled, and sang my songs
of praise for the gift of children!

Forgive all my complaining, Jesus. I really do love being a
parent — even on Sundays!

I love you. Amen.

A Friend Is . . .

"Friends look pretty and are always pretty inside."

"Friends look like they love each other."

"Friends cost nothing, you can't buy them."

"Jesus is my best friend."

"The person you like the most in the whole wide
world is your friend."

A friend loves at all times. [Prov. 17:17]

Dear Jesus,

Talking to you, my best and most understanding friend,
always helps to relieve my frustrations and put
life in perspective!

You listen and love me when I am angry because I heard my
children being called names by their friends!

You listen and love me when I feel the storm brewing inside
because other adults were criticizing my children!

You listen and love me when I am grouchy because there is
not enough of me to go around when all the children
need help with mountains of homework!

And, you even love me when I am so proud of
them I could burst!

Through good and bad, your friendship is always there.

Lord Jesus, bless my children with good friends.
Lead them to experience the special friendship that only they and you can share together!

I love you for the gift of children. Amen.

Grass Is Green, How Does It Get That Way?

"Jesus does it."

"It rains."

"The snow melts and you get green grass that way."

"When you feed grass it gets green."

The grass withers and the flowers fall,
  but the word of our God stands forever. [Isa. 40:8]

Dear Father,

Children love to play hide-and-seek. As I watch them run here and there, shouting, "You can't find me," I can't help but think about their future and the things I, as a Christian parent, want to teach them while they are still in my home.

Help me to joyfully teach them your Word. Lead them to take these words and hide them in their hearts, so they will know no matter where they go . . . taking a bike ride, fighting a war, cutting paper dolls, or building space rockets . . . your Word is always with them.

Thank you, Father, for the gift of children and for the opportunity to hide Your word in our hearts as a reservoir of instant strength throughout our lives. I love you. Amen.

Flu, I Know All about It!

You get the flu from bugs that . . .

"live in trees."
"under the
ground."
"in the air."
"look like a big
giant web."

"Flu bugs eat snow, grass, and when they eat mud
they get their insides all muddy."

"You can get rid of the flu bugs by getting a big fly
swatter and zapping them real good!"

"You can get rid of them by stepping on them,
taking yucky medicine, or smacking them
with both hands."

"You can keep from getting the flu bug by drinking
lots of super fly medicine to keep him away
or keeping a great big net over you so the
old bug can't get you!"

Many . . . are the wonders you have done. [Ps. 40:5]

Dear Jesus,
It is a terrifying experience when my children are sick with
very high fevers!
All I can think of is — brain damage!

The doctor tells me to remain calm!
Throughout the night I use wet towels to cool my
child.
How I wish I would be the one who is sick.

I look at my child and feel so helpless.
There is nothing I can humanly do.
Only you, my great Physician,

can perform the miracle
on my child.

I praise you every day for the unlimited miracles you perform
in the lives of my children.

Yet,
when there is sickness,
I totally surrender to your will!

I know that my life is nothing without you.
With you, all things are possible.

Thank you for the gift of children,
and especially for the wonders only you can perform!
I love you. Amen.

Tell Me about Old People

"People are old when they look like your grandmas
and grandpas."

"People are old when they stand on the thing with
lots of numbers and it tells them how old
they are."

"When people look real, real, real old — they are!"

"You know someone is old when they have a cane."

"You're old when you hurt all the time."

"People are old when they are ready for heaven,
about ninety-nine."

He has made everything beautiful in its time.
[Eccles. 3:11]

Dear Jesus,

From my children's point of view, "old" is only a few years
older than they are! I think I felt that way once too!

Even though my body may grow older, dear Jesus,
keep me young in the desire to learn more about you . . .
give me a bubbly personality to eagerly share the
miracles you perform in my "old age" . . .
and the appreciation of the individual uniqueness of
children!

No matter what my age, make me a beautiful servant of yours
so that my children will look forward to each
stage of their life.

I love you for the gift of children —
no matter what my age! Amen.

Who Taught Mommy and Daddy How to Spank?

"Grandmas and grandpas."

"God."

"God taught the first moms and dads."

He who spares the rod hates his son,
*   but he who loves him is careful to discipline him.*
        [Prov. 13:24]

Lord Jesus,

   Disciplining my children is not something I enjoy doing,
      yet I get a lot of practice!

      I quickly send my child to his room for lying about the
         unfinished homework I found pitched in the waste-
            basket!

            I do not hesitate to slap my daughter's little fingers
               when she is playing with the buttons on our
               new TV!

               I irresponsibly take away privileges when they
                  fight about picking up their toys!

   Jesus, I try to be consistent and treat each child equally.
      But it isn't always easy to do!

         I feel as if I should receive the award for worst parent
            of the year.

Thank you for being the perfect parent, Father, for always being consistent with me, your child.

Help me as I discipline my children.

I love you, Lord Jesus, for the gift of children even when I do need to correct them. Amen.

Babies

"Babies come from mommies and mommies come from God."

"My mom had surgery and then she got the baby out. The doctor pushed a little door and the baby just came out. The baby had a bellybutton with a plug attached, so the doctor snapped the cord with a scissors. You know, babies grow in a sack in the mom's tummy like you get at the grocery store, a brown one. Jesus tells the baby when it is time to go to the hospital because the mommy gets really fat and they just have to come out!"

"To get a baby, first they cut in the stomach and God puts a seed in to get a baby and it stays there until Mother's Day. Then you go to the hospital and lay down on the floor. Next they do a touch-up with hands. They relax and think nice thoughts (like sleepin'). You breathe special out of your nose and the mouth at the same time. Then they just pull out the baby and put back in the stomach!"

"To get a baby they first cut a little dip on her stomach and it just pops out!"

"Moms come from moms and dads come from moms too!"

"I have two sisters. One came from Mommy and
    one came from Daddy."

"God puts bones in babies so they will stick together
    and then he breathes on them."

"My sister is bigger than I am 'cause she was borned
    first."

"Babies talk when they cry."

"Babies cry so they can grow strong."

---

*Like newborn babies, crave pure spiritual milk, so that by it
you may grow up in your salvation, now that you have
tasted that the Lord is good.* [1 Peter 2:2]

Dear loving Creator,
    As I look at my newborn baby for the first time, I am in awe!
        Only you could create such a beautiful, complete,
        functioning human being!

My mind quickly races through my child's life . . .
    Will I be a good parent?
    Will my child be healthy?
    What will my child be when he grows up?
    What will my child's family be like?
    Where will they live?

It seems this tiny, helpless infant will be in my life forever.
    Yet, I know, Creator, that someday my child will be leaving
        me.

Lord, help me to make the best of the time you have planned for
        us together.
    My eyes fill with tears of joy. I praise you, wonderful Creator,
        for the gift of a child! I love you. Amen.

I Know All about Diseases

"Chicken pox you get from chickens, of course."

"You get rid of chicken pox by putting corn powder on them. They last for two days and you get the pox when you bite people."

"Heart murmurs . . . it's just like a little stomachache."

"Measles . . . you don't get them anymore, because you get animal shots so you won't get them."

A cheerful heart is good medicine. [Prov. 17:22]

Dear Jesus,
The question is: should I or should I not take my child to the doctor? I see spots again!

This seems to be the umpteenth time this has happened.
Could it be measles or chicken pox this time?
If only I knew what to do!

  The unknowns in life frighten me . . .
    I wonder, will I always be around to care for my children?
        will I be able to make each individual child feel loved and special?
        will I give equal amounts of my time to each child so no one will feel cheated?

I am thankful, dear Jesus, that only you know the answers to my questions!

Help me to willingly submit to your will and allow you to totally control my thoughts and actions! Help me to joyfully step out in faith and accept the unknown as a way of showing I trust you.

Fill my heart with the medicine of praise so my children will see me radiate dependence on you!

Thank you for the gift of children, in whom I can see your almighty powers performed. I love you. Amen.

What Is a Family?

"They eat supper together and have fun together."

"I don't know what a family is, but I know I have one at home."

"They sit down and watch the news."

"A family is when everyone is together."

"A family is a mother and a father and something that's fun."

"A family is people who love each other."

"Families are people who take turns washing dishes."

"A family is people who put kids to bed and parents stay up."

And God blessed them, and God said to them, "Be fruitful and multiply, and fill the earth and subdue it. . . ."
[Gen. 1:26, RSV]

Dear God,
  You said it!
    Everything you made was good!
      I agree!
        Aren't children the neatest people?

  I love their hugs and kisses, the "I love yous."
    Yet my heart pains as I know this time of having
    children in our home will swiftly pass.

Please bless my children with happy, healthy families.
Show them how wonderful your gift of children really is!

I love you. Amen.

When Do Your Parents Kiss?

"Only on Sundays or Fridays."

"When Dad comes home from work they always kiss."

"All the time."

"At 10:00 every night."

"When it gets dark."

Jesus Christ is the same yesterday and today and forever.
[Heb. 13:8]

Dear beautiful Savior,
   I am not sure I like to see the change in my children as they grow older!

When they were little they loved to sit on my lap and we would
   cuddle close to each other and give lots of hugs and kisses.
      Now that they are older, their idea of kissing a parent is
         something you do only when no one else is around!

Jesus, I am glad you never change the way we do.
   To know you love each one of us as much today
   as you did yesterday is exciting.

To believe you will love us tomorrow as much as you
love us today is beyond my comprehension!

Thank you, Jesus, for the gift of children.
I can feel you loving me through them!
I love you too. Amen.

What Do You Know about Mothers?

"They are supposed to cook and take care of
children that come from God and kick their
way out of her tummy."

*Let the words of my mouth and the meditation of my heart,
be acceptable in thy sight,
O LORD, my rock and my redeemer.* [Ps. 19:14, RSV]

Precious Savior,

It was finally time to sit down in my favorite rocker and rest!
Today had been an
exciting day. I had worked for hours getting the perfect
flower bed
planted, lovingly watered the little seedlings, and
looked
forward to the beauty that would surround my home
until . . .
I noticed the children were unusually quiet!
Could it be they fell asleep?

As I went back outside to investigate their whereabouts, I discovered they
too were having an exciting time in the freshly planted flower
bed!

As I watched them giggle and squeeze mud between their fingers
and toes . . .
   lovingly give the delicate seedlings huge drinks of water from
   an old cup . . .
      I wanted to yell: "Get out of there! Don't you know I've
      spent hours trying to make our yard pretty, spent a lot of
      money on those seeds, and now you have ruined it!"

But, I prayed, *"God help me!"*
   In that moment you helped me experience the gift of children,
      and only you, precious Savior, gave me the patience I
      needed
         to see the true beauty that surrounds my home all sea-
         sons of the year!

Thank you, Savior, for letting me see that life with children is like
a beautiful garden. You plant them in the world. You allow me
to be the gardener and tend your crop,

                    nourish it,
                    care for it,
                    help to weed out the sins of life,
                    see the tender little seedlings grow
                       and bloom for the purpose you
                       have planned for them in life.

I love you for the gift of children and I pray our words and
thoughts will always be acceptable in your sight. Amen.

Tell Me about Baptism, What Does It Mean?

"Every time I get into the bathtub, I get bathized."

"It's when they don't hold your nose and everyone comes to see you go under the water."

"It's God building you up."

"Bathized, it's what you do just before you brush your teeth and go to bed."

"Baptism means you get your head wet 'cause you believe in God."

"That's what makes me cold. I got water threw all over my head once."

"Baptized means when you get your hair wet then you are God's child."

"It's a way of thanking him 'cause you love him."

"It's when you get your head wet so you can grow up."

"'Rise and be baptized, and wash away your sins.'"
[Acts 22:16, RSV]

Loving Jesus,
    It is a feeling of accomplishment to put my child, who is

covered with mud and sand from head to toe, in the tub of
water
and eventually see a clean, glowing child!

I am reminded of my baptism and that of my children . . .
how our dirty lives can be washed clean through your
Word. Keep me ever mindful of my baptism and of your
love.

I love you, Jesus, for the gift of making us your children! Amen.

How Do Your Prayers Get to God?

"My prayers fly out the window and up to him in the sky."

"Prayers get to him by rocket."

"Prayers all go up to God when I go to sleep at night."

"God has bionic ears."

"You have to talk real loud for him to hear way up there."

"He just puts his ear down on a cloud and listens real close."

"God's very special. He picks up all our prayers and then records them, then he sits down and listens to them."

"An airplane takes them up to heaven."

"You jump on the trampoline and they bounce up to him."

"If you ask anything in my name, I will do it."
[John 14:14, RSV]

Dear Jesus,
Thank you for listening to the simple,
uncomplicated prayers of my children.

As I hear their prayers
   I am quickly taken from my adult world
      and delightfully grow in my love for you
         through their childlike faith!

Thank you for the gift of children who help me come to you and tell it like it is! I love you. Amen.

What Is a Mirror?

"It's a thing on the bathroom door."

"It's for shaving."

"It's to see how pretty God made you."

"It's so you can look at yourself and yourself can look back."

"It's to see if you are all dressed or not."

"It's to tell you if you like what you see and if you don't you start all over."

"You use it so you will know how other people will see you."

I praise you because I am fearfully and wonderfully made; your works are wonderful. . . .
[Ps. 139:14]

Dear Creator,

You know the feelings I have about myself when I look into a mirror!

You know the feelings my children experience as they are maturing into young adults!

I am unhappy because I have gained weight since the birth of my last child.

My children are unhappy because they are not maturing to
full size . . .
instantly . . . like "everyone else!"

I complain because my hair is too short and curly or long and
straight.
They complain because their nose is not the right size or
they have two freckles on their left arm!

Remind us, Creator, that each time we look into a mirror, we
reflect your wonderful creation!
You knew exactly how *you* wanted each of us to look — even
to the last smile line on our faces!

Thank you, Creator of all, for the gift of children and for
making each one of them different to express your unique
blessings of creation.
I love you. Amen.

What Does Jesus Look Like and What Does He Do?

"He has a mustache, is tall and skinny. He helps you
get better if you're sick."

"He has a beard, blue eyes, and white shirt."

"He makes people alive in heaven."

"He does all kinds of good stuff for you."

"He's preparing a place for us when we die."

"He has a happy face!"

"He makes it rain from the sky."

"He wears brown boots."

"He puts you together in heaven."

A wise son brings joy to his father. [Prov. 10:1]

Dear Jesus,
You must be a very joyful person!
Smiling.
Laughing.
How can you help but be that way when you look at
the beautiful children you created . . .
watch their funny little antics . . .
listen to their unique comments about life in
the adults' world!

You know everything about us —
   where we go,
   what we do,
      every single thought we think!

Thank you for forgiving our sins, for loving us as we are.
Help me to bring joy to my children and to you.

I love you for the gift of children. Amen.

What Is a Sunday School?

"Someplace you pray so the people upstairs can't
hear you."

Come, my children, listen to me;
  I will teach you the fear of the LORD. [Ps. 34:11]

Loving Savior,
  Help me to create a happy atmosphere in my home —
    especially on Sundays!

  Give my children an extra ounce of patience to sit
    still in class.
  Bless the teachers who contend with endless questions . . .
                    wiggles . . .
                      impatience . . .
  Thank you, Savior, for the gift of children who grow
    in their love for you in many ways!
        I love you too! Amen.

What Is a Christian?

"A man who goes to church and tells about God."

"When you're in church you are a Christian."

"It's the name of someone."

"It means you get stuff."

"I think it's a football and gets kicked around and tossed."

A happy heart makes the face cheerful. . . . [Prov. 15:13]

Dear Lord, Creator of my children,
  Most of the time
    I smile because you live in my heart and motivate my total being,
  but there are times, Father, when it is difficult to smile!

Such as the time I served snacks of raisins, peanuts, and coconut and they were spilled into the shag carpet . . .
    or when I try to keep the little hands out of the candy and gum while I'm unloading the grocery cart at the checkout.

I know, though, that being a Christian is following you and dealing with my children in loving ways!

Help me to always find good in everything they do.
Help me to keep the smile on my face and the joy in my
heart,
because I know these children were especially chosen
for me, by you!

I love you for the gift of my children. Amen.

What Is Communion?

"It is a meeting to have dinner and come home late
'cause you ate too much."

"Someone who works on a telephone line."

"It's when you get something up in front at church
like bread."

"It means you get to eat in church with God that
day."

---

*"Come to me, all who labor and are heavy laden, and I will
give you rest."* [Matt. 11:28, RSV]

Dear Father,

Do you realize how hard it is to rear children and create
a happy home?

I guess you must — after all, I am one of your children!

It's wonderful to know, Father, that you can really identify
with the joys and frustrations in my life.

Today I spent most of the day cleaning house and tonight it
looks as if I never touched it! Sometimes I feel,

"What's the use!"

Yet today, one of my children shared a very special secret
with me. Wow!

Thank you, Father, for letting me communicate with you,
for the gifts of forgiveness and strength
to meet the needs of my children.

I love you for the gift of children even in times
of frustration! Amen.

I Can Tell You All about the Devil!

The devil . . .

> "does not get paid because he is bad."
>
> "tells people to mess up their rooms."
>
> "tells people to hit me."
>
> "makes you do bad things."
>
> "lives in a hole under my sandbox."
>
> "has red hair, eats mud 'cause he is dirty, and likes to sin."
>
> "is mean 'cause he doesn't do what Jesus says."
>
> "has something on his back that helps him fly like Superman but doesn't have a Superman pants or voice."
>
> "eats dirty, moldy sandwiches, dark foods, worms, and candy."
>
> "goes up and down in an underground elevator to hell."

When I was a child, I talked like a child, I thought like a child, I reasoned like a child. When I became a man, I put childish ways behind me. [1 Cor. 13:11]

Dear Lord of all,
  Do not let the devil tempt me into taking advantage of
    my children by getting them involved in so many social
      activities, for self-pride, that we forget to put
        you first in our lives!

Help me, Lord, to resist the devil and all his ways as
  I mold the children you have given to me.

      I love you. Amen.

Jesus Came to My House One Day!

"Jesus came to my house. He played with me all the time when I was up. Sometimes he gets busy and he has to do his work. Jesus always loves me. He looks like a little boy and is sorta fat. He eats angel food cake. He lives a long way from here. He goes and does his paperwork on my dad's typewriter and at my dad's desk. He makes everyone in the whole wide world happy."

Tell it to your children,
*   and let your children tell it to their children,*
*   and their children to the next generation.* [Joel 1:3]

Dear God,

I often wonder what my children will tell their children about our home and about me.

Will they remember how I reacted when . . .

I found the half roll of Charmin stuffed in the toilet?

I received a very important phone call and they let World War III erupt at my feet?

they giggled because my hands were always wet when they needed their pants snapped and zipped?

it was Sunday morning and six people were sharing one bathroom?

Or, will they remember . . .

how much I wanted them to know all about you.

the many times I prayed for them.

how I longed for them to love to worship in church
and have fun at youth activities.

a happy home where they felt loved and accepted.

my smiles, laughter, and joyful witness I could
not control because it was my way of
praising you for the gift of children.

Thank you, God, for giving us a happy home and healthy children and for living in our homes and hearts every day. I love you. Amen.

What Are Germs?

"They are things you eat for supper if you don't
wash."

"Rusty-colored things that get in your mouth."

"Germs are things that make holes in your teeth."

Germs are something you give to other people that
aren't presents."

"Germs are things that get in your nose."

"Germs have black legs and a black stomach and
black eyes . . . and make you sneeze!"

"They eat you and look like yuk."

"They are purple and look like somebody I know."

---

*Now faith is being sure of what we hope for and certain of
what we do not see.* [Heb. 11:1]

Dear Father,

My children have a million questions that need answers . . .
all at once . . . and always — right away!

They question why they should wash their hands before eat-
ing,
why they should cover their mouths when they cough,
when the flower they planted will grow,
how long until their birthday.

If only I could be more like my children and gladly accept
through faith
the answers to all my questions in life!

I praise you, loving Father, for all the things I have seen that
prove you love me, and for all the things I have not yet
seen . . .
and for always keeping your word!

Help my children learn what faith is through
my witness
of you in my life.

Thank you for the gift of children.
I have faith you will always keep them in your care!
I love you. Amen.

When Does Your Mommy Love You?

"When it's Christmas."

"Always."

"Only in the mornings when I get up."

"When I put pretty clothes on."

"She loves me when I clean my room."

"She loves me all the time, 'cause I'm her child."

"Well, not when I'm naughty."

Dear friends, let us love one another, for love comes from God. [1 John 4:7]

Dear Jesus,
    It's easy to tell the children I love them when they are
        helping with the cleaning,
           being good,
                getting good grades in school,
                    taking part in the school program.
But then there are other times when it isn't as easy . . .
when it's mealtime and everyone is hungry and grouchy and
    the food isn't ready yet.
when the children are tired and picking on each other before
        bedtime!

when I've finally had the opportunity to make some extra money, lined up a sitter, was ready to leave, and one child got up sick. Should I stay home and be a mommy or should I go to work and hope she doesn't get worse?

Lord Jesus, don't ever let me run out of love, no matter what the situation for any of my children. Help me to let them know that I do not like sins they commit, but my love for them will always be there.

I love you, dear Jesus, for the gift of children
and the opportunity you give to me to pass on the love you put into my heart! Amen.

Tell Me What You Know about a Preacher or a Priest

"They wear girls' dresses, talk a lot, and put white
towels around their necks."

"He is someone who takes all your money in church
and talks church talk."

"They tell people when to sing and when to stand up
and sit down."

"They are Jesus' messengers and wear Jesus
clothes."

"Preachers come out of the church first on Sundays."

"Preachers stay in the church and wait for people to
come."

"They make Jesus happy."

---

*Train a child in the way he should go,
and when he is old he will not turn from it.*
[Prov. 22:6]

Dear Father,
　　Sometimes I feel like a preacher!
　　　　I preach about junk foods . . .
　　　　I preach about picking up toys . . .
　　　　I preach about the miracle it will take to once again
　　　　　　see carpet under the beds . . .

I preach about wearing thongs outside in zero-degree
weather . . .

I get so absorbed in little insignificant incidents in life I often
forget the real sermon I am to preach for you.

Father, you know how much help I need

> every day
> to train my chil-
> dren to give you
> all glory . . .

to allow you to be the exciting, motivating force in their
lives.

Most of all, let my sermon be through my actions, to keep you at
the center of every day of my life.

> I love you, Father, for the gift of watching children grow
> up. Amen.

Love

"God puts love inside your body when you are
 born."

"Love is something that makes you feel all smiley
 inside."

"If you kiss someone and hug them then you'll know
 if you're in love."

"Love is when you get a drink of water for
 somebody."

"Love is when first God made an egg, but it's not
 white, then it is hatched, then the baby
 comes out."

"Love is marriage when you walk with your hands
 hooked together."

"You get love from your best friends."

"Love is when you get married, people just go
 someplace and the pastor says something and
 then they go beep the horns."

"Love is when Mommy hugs me."

"I have loved you with an everlasting love."
 [Jer. 31:3, RSV]

Dear Lord,

Thank you for letting me be able to naturally tell my children "I love you" . . .

> not just at bedtime, but any time of the day,
>
> no matter where we are,
>
> or who is around!

Thank you for letting me be able to freely express the love you put into my heart, through smiles . . .

> winks . . .
>
> even hugs!

I love you, Lord of my life, for the gift of my children and the ability to love even in their unlovable moments! Amen.

Tell Me Something Special about Your Grandmother

"When I go to her house she does magic tricks. She has magic teeth. She takes them out and puts them back in again."

Children's children are a crown to the aged, and parents are the pride of their children. [Prov. 17:6]

Dear Lord of goodness,
   You must wear a big smile on your face every time a grandparent says to someone, "Do you want to see a picture of my grandchild? I just happen to have one!"

The precious moments that you give to children and grandparents are priceless events
   that can never be erased from a memory!

Grandparents become alive when they interact with their grandkids . . .
   playing "old-fashioned" games . . .
   talking about the "good old days" . . .

I love you, Lord, for the gift of children and the times children and grandparents can experience each other! Amen.

I Can Tell You Why My Family Needs Me!

"To give them kisses and hugs."

"Daddy needs me so I can carry in the wood."

"They need me so I can clean up my messy room."

"They need me 'cause they need someone to read stories to."

"Daddy needs me so he will have someone to ask him questions."

"A family needs kids so they can clear off the table and do the dishes."

"They need me 'cause they need someone to put the dog out and carry out trash."

"They need someone to give their love to."

Glory in his holy name;
let the hearts of those who seek the LORD rejoice!
[Ps. 105:3]

Dear heavenly Father,
Help me to always let my children know I need them.
Forgive me for the times when I want to be alone,
when I want time for just me,

when I shut them out of my
thoughts!

Father, my heart leaps for joy when I think of the
wonderful things you do in my life, and for giving me ways
to show my children I need them and I want them to
need me.

I love you for the gift of children. Amen.

Why Do You Take a Bath?

"Because Mom says you gotta take one or you'll get
   your bed dirty."

"To get your insides clean."

"So you smell good."

"So I can come to school."

"So you get warm."

"If you don't take a bath you'll stink and everybody
   will get away from you."

"To get money."

Rejoice in the Lord always; again I will say, Rejoice.
   [Phil. 4:4, RSV]

Dear Jesus,
   There are times I could just scream!
   Why is it that I can get the children bathed, dressed in clean
clothes, ready to go away and

in the few seconds it takes me
to get ready they become a
magnet for mud! From the
top of their heads to the bot-
tom of their toes!

   At times like this, I wonder, how can I always rejoice?

Yet,

I know my children have more clean clothes . . .

I have water to bathe them in . . .

I have healthy children who can run and play and get dirty.

Jesus, if I made a list of all the things I can rejoice about in my
life, I would never have time to be a parent . . . the list would
never end!

Each year

      month

        week

          day

            hour

              minute

                second

                  you shower me with abundant blessings.
                  More blessings than I can ever compre-
                  hend!

Help me to always look for good in everything that happens to
  me and my children.
    Help me to remain calm in times of crises
      and count my blessings — instead of yelling!

I love you, Jesus, for the gift of children — dirty or clean! Amen.

My Favorite Bible Story

While teaching the creation story in school one day,
I had just told the children that God made
Adam and Eve. One young child excitedly
yelled out, "I know Adam, he's my cousin!"

"Blessed rather are those who hear the word of God and keep it!" [Luke 11:28, RSV]

Dear Lord God, Author of the Scriptures,
help me to always make your Word come alive
   and be a real part of my children's lives!

Thank you for the gift of your Word and children
   I can read it to!

   I love you. Amen.

"Dear God" Letters

"Dear God, when is the next football game?"

"Dear God, did you ever have a shot? I'm getting one on Friday and it will feel like Mommy pinching me."

"Dear God, I would like to go to the moon so I can see you. I could bring a big bag of food and we could have a picnic on a cloud."

"Dear God, have a wonderful day today. Just don't make any more people like me 'cause you made me special. I love you, God."

"Dear God, how do you make bugs turn into butterflies?"

"Dear God, how do you make people and animals? It must be hard work thinkin' up so many different kinds of people and animals."

"Dear God, I love you because you are sweet to me."

Ask in faith, with no doubting. [James 1:6, RSV]

Dear God,
    Will my children ever grow up?
        Today I was
    correcting them for decorating the kitchen
        cupboards with felt-tipped markers . . .

scolding them for forgetting to watch the new puppy —
oops, another puddle on the carpet . . .
waiting in line at the grocery for ten minutes and having
to leave the line because one child positively could wait
no longer to go to the bathroom!

I have no doubts that you will bless their growth,
But in the meantime,
would you please give me guidance and
wisdom to train my children without so
much stress?

Even today, God, I love you for the gift of children! Amen.

Things I Know about Santa

"Santa doesn't get his beard dirty because he is very careful how he goes down the chimney."

"Santa washes his beard before he goes to the next house."

"Santa gets his beard dirty on the way down, but it gets clean on the way up."

"Santa uses a rag and Coast soap to wash it."

"If the elves don't get the right pieces in the right places, Santa leaves us a note and tells us to make their mistakes right."

"He just touches his nose and presto — he's magical and up he goes."

"He uses a telephone pole to help him get up and down the chimny."

"Santa is fat because he eats too much junk food."

"Santa wouldn't be Santa if he wouldn't be fat!"

Dear children, let us not love with words or tongue but with actions and in truth. [1 John 3:18]

Dear Father,
   Forgive me for carelessly letting myself get sucked into the whirlpool of worldly pressures at Christmas.

I think I "must" entertain . . .
>I "must" bake . . .
>I "must" decorate . . .
>I "must" spend a lot of money to buy everyone the gifts
>>they "must" have . . .
>I "must" allow the commercial Santa to be part of our
>excitement.

Help me, Father, to put this exciting season into perspective!
>I enjoy doing things for others,
>>giving to others,
>>>because I am excited over the great event that happened
>>>>long ago,
>>>your only Son's birth.

Help me to set the tone for my family through my words and
>actions . . .
>this happiness we feel is not of Santa giving presents
>but
>>because of your Son's birthday!

Give me wisdom, Father, to create special memories for the children to remember the way we celebrated your gift to us. Then guide my children to continue making Jesus the center of their own homes' celebrations.

>Thank you for the gift of children.
>>They are exciting!
>>>I love you. Amen.

Tell Me about the Tooth Fairy

"It looks like an angel."

"The fairy wears a Cinderella dress."

"The tooth fairy comes to the house on a broom like a witch."

"The fairy lives in a tooth house."

"She uses our teeth for candles on her birthday cake."

"He's invisible."

"She hides under your bed."

"The fairy gets her money from the bank in the clouds."

. . . *put your trust in the LORD.* . . . [Ps. 4:5, RSV]

Dear Jesus,
  I have fun pretending to be the tooth fairy,
                              the Easter Bunny,
                              Santa Claus.
  And yet, it bothers me that my children may not be able to separate make-believe from the real thing.

  Give me wisdom, Jesus, to impress upon their absorbent minds that you are for real!

Let them be little sponges and soak up the fact that through
you alone is eternal life.
Thank you, Jesus, for the gift of children and the gift of
eternal life! I love you. Amen.

What Is a Gall Bladder?

"I know exactly what a gall bladder is. It is someone
with a bat, you know, like a gall batter on a
baseball team!"

---

*From him the whole body, joined and held together by every
supporting ligament, grows and builds itself up in love, as
each part does its work.* [Eph. 4:16]

Dear Father,
   It is getting very difficult to function as a family unit
   as the children grow older. This scares me!

We used to enjoy reading and playing games together, singing
songs, and making goodies in the kitchen.
   Now we seem to each be pulled in different directions —
   sports, after-school activities, parties, dates, jobs.

When they were little they competed for attention.
   I would hear, "You helped her ride her bike longer than you
            helped me build my model airplane!"
   Now I hear, "You bought her more new clothes than me" or
      "You let him stay out later."

Help me, God of my life, to find ways to keep my
family unit strong.

Open new doors, and make it obvious how we can minister
to each other's needs and build each other up.
Never let us drift from showing affection,
hugs,
kisses,
"I love yous,"
no matter how old we get!

Thank you, Father, for the gift of children who help to make
my family complete! I love you. Amen.

What Do You Think These Terms Mean?

Bedpan: "Bedpan is a tray you eat on when you are really sick and can't go to the table to eat."

Hypochondriac: "A person at the hospital who paints the walls."

Injection: "When two roads come together."

Vein: "Something where you can't walk right, it's right behind your knee and down to the heel and a daddy can fix it with a big bandage."

Surgeon: "It's like operating on a body, they have a mirror to shine on a body and if they see something, they take it out."

Mental health: "It means if you eat too many mints it will not be healthy."

Nurses' station: "Where nurses go to get gas."

Gynecologist: "A person who plays a guitar in a hospital."

Let the word of Christ dwell in you richly as you teach and admonish one another. [Col. 3:16]

Dear Jesus,
I love to listen to the cute things my children say!
They give long, detailed explanations about things of which

88

they have no concept. I know my eyes must twinkle,
and I must smile from ear to ear, rejoicing in being the
parent of these darling children!

Give me wisdom, when I read your Word to my children, to
explain it in terms they can understand.
Then
show me how
to follow up with actions
that make plain the meaning of your Word.

Let your Word be a bright light, the motivating factor for
every second of our lives.

Thank you, Jesus, for the gift of children and for making your
Word exciting!

I love you. Amen.

Glossary of Cooking Terms

Baste: "to run to base."

Bone: "to break it, like when you break your leg or cut it."

Broil: "to cook over water."

Cream: "to squeeze it."

Cube: "to put something on an ice cube."

Grate: "that means good."

Knead: "that's like when you need someone."

Give thanks to the LORD . . . who gives food to every creature. [Ps. 136:1, 25]

Dear Jesus,
    I try very hard to make mealtime a happy, joyful experience.
        I want it to be a time the entire family looks forward to.
            A time when we can share the events of the day . . .
                grow physically through the food you give to us . . .
                grow spiritually through our family devotions.
    And you know, too, Jesus, how frustrated I feel when these
    things do not happen.

    Why is it the kids want to watch TV at mealtime?
    Why is it they spill milk over my freshly mopped and waxed
        floor?

Why is it the telephone rings or someone knocks at the door
during devotions?
Why is it the children take hours to dawdle over nutritious
foods and only seconds to devour a bag of candy or
cookies?

Show me how, Lord, to joyfully take advantage of the minutes
we do have together as a family.
Help us establish the habit of thanking you for the food you
provide for our nourishment, whether it is a meal together at
home . . .
on a picnic . . .
at the fast-food shop . . .
and yes, even when we have a little snack!

Thank you, Jesus, for the gift of children and for the
opportunity to help them acknowledge that you give
us everything we need for life.
I love you. Amen.

Tell Me about Hospitals, Nurses, and X Rays

X ray: "It's something you use to take a beard off."

"It's for broken arms — to give the doctors a
picture of it."

"It is so they can see what's in your body, like
what you had for dinner."

Nurses: "They make you better and wear crossed
hats."

"They are doctors that real doctors tell what to do
and where to go."

"They take babies out of mommies."

"Hospitals are . . . big buildings with nurses and
doctors and lots of presents. They are built
with bricks, have lots of rooms, and give
shots there."

Emergency-room equipment: "It's called a stella-
scope or a tella-scope."

The Lord is my helper; I will not be afraid. [Heb. 13:6]

Dear great Physician,
The children were having so much fun, giggling, climbing, act-
ing silly —
then it happened!

I heard the chilling scream. The next thing I saw was
blood gushing from my child's forehead.
Help, God! We are on our way to the hospital emergency room!

The seconds seemed like hours.
What were the doctors and nurses doing to my child?

My palms were wet and clammy. I shifted endlessly in my seat.
My mind raced back and forth over the look on the nurses'
faces.
I shamefully wondered if they would know exactly how to
repair this kind of wound.

I look to you, great Physician, for I know you are the one in
control.
You did not go to school for more than twenty years to learn
how to treat most kinds of accidents. You are all-
knowing!
Qualified to handle the most serious to the most
minute detail in our lives!

I relax, as I once again recognize your greatness.
I experience a calmness flowing through my body.
I never need to be afraid, for you are with me and my child,
the doctors and nurses.

You can
and do
perform miracles!

Thank you, Dr. Jesus, for the gift of children and
for the tender loving ways you touch our lives
second
by second!
I love you. Amen.